I SPY
Numbers in Art

For Walter and Molly

FOREWORD

Young children have an insatiable appetite for picture books. They are happy to spend hour after hour looking and learning and are always anxious for more. When pictures are still a major source of entertainment for children this is the time to introduce them to art. Each image will be studied and explored and, while some may be dismissed, a great many will be relished and remembered.

When my own children were tiny, they loved looking at the pictures in a book of medieval paintings. They were fascinated by the minute details and the rich colours and patterns. Over the years we have looked at hundreds of pictures from all over the world and I hope you will enjoy the twenty I have chosen for this book. They are all paintings except for one, which is a beautiful Japanese woodblock print.

I dedicate this book to my children without whom I would never have thought of it.

Lucy Micklethwait 1992

Cover picture: Henri Matisse, *Goldfish* (1911)
Title page picture: Henri Rousseau, *Artillerymen* (about 1893-1895)

I SPY
Numbers in Art

Devised & selected by Lucy Micklethwait

HarperCollins *Children's Books*

I spy
one fly

1

GEBORNE HOFERIN,

I spy
two eyes

2

Karel Appel, *Cry for Freedom*

I spy
three puppies

3

I spy
four fish

4

Henri Matisse, *Goldfish*

I spy
five eggs

5

Jan van Huijsum, *Flowers in a Terracotta Vase*

I spy
six ducks

6

Utagawa Kuniyoshi, *Boat Trip in Winter*

I spy
seven circles

7

Wassily Kandinsky, *Swinging*

I spy
eight boats

8

Vincent Van Gogh, *Boats on the Beach*

I spy
nine children

9

Studio of Peter Paul Rubens, *The Gerbier Family*

I spy
ten hens

10

Sir Stanley Spencer, *St. Francis and the Birds*

I spy
eleven hares

11

Unknown artist, *The Emblem of the Hare*

I spy
twelve squirrels

12

Abu'l Hasan, *Squirrels in a Plane Tree*

I spy
thirteen singers

13

Thomas Cooper Gotch, *Alleluia*

I spy
fourteen soldiers

14

Henri Rousseau, *Artillerymen*

I spy
fifteen hands and feet

15

Fernand Léger, *Divers on a Yellow Background*

I spy
sixteen apples

16

Lucas Cranach the Elder, *Madonna and Child under an Apple Tree*

I spy
seventeen birds

17

Pablo Picasso, *The New Year*

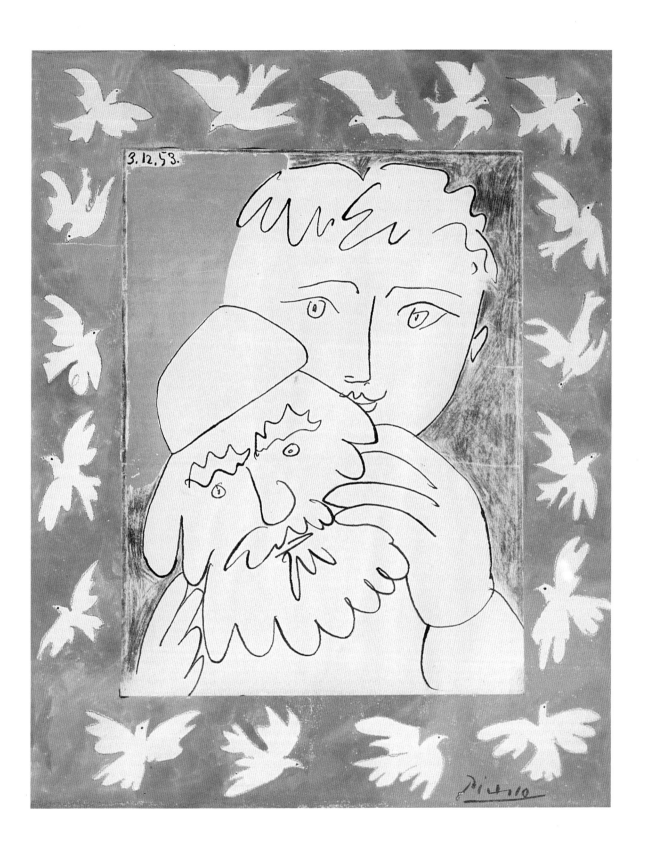

I spy
eighteen cherries

18

Georg Flegel, *Still Life*

I spy
nineteen stars

19

Robert Indiana, *The American Dream I* (1961)

I spy
twenty angels

20

Sandro Botticelli, *Mystic Nativity*

— I Spied Numbers in Art —

1 one fly
Swabian School (15th Century), *Portrait of a Woman of the Hofer Family*
The National Gallery, London

2 two eyes
Karel Appel (born 1921), *Cry for Freedom* (1948)
N.V. Koninklijke Bijenkorf Beheer KBB, Amsterdam

3 three puppies
Paul Gauguin (1848-1903), *Still Life with Three Puppies* (1888)
The Museum of Modern Art, New York
Mrs. Simon Guggenheim Fund

4 four fish
Henri Matisse (1869-1954), *Goldfish* (1911)
Pushkin Museum, Moscow

5 five eggs
Jan van Huijsum (1682-1749), *Flowers in a Terracotta Vase* (1736-1737)
The National Gallery, London

6 six ducks
Utagawa Kuniyoshi (1797-1861), *Boat Trip in Winter* (about 1853)
Van Gogh Museum, Amsterdam

7 seven circles
Wassily Kandinsky (1866-1944), *Swinging* (1925)
The Tate Gallery, London

8 eight boats

Vincent Van Gogh (1853-1890), *Boats on the Beach* (1888)

Van Gogh Museum, Amsterdam

9 nine children

Studio of Peter Paul Rubens (1577-1640), *The Gerbier Family* (about 1630)

The Royal Collection, St. James's Palace, London

10 ten hens

Sir Stanley Spencer (1891-1959), *St. Francis and the Birds* (1935)

The Tate Gallery, London

11 eleven hares

Unknown artist, *The Emblem of the Hare* from *Le Livre de la Chasse*

(about 1405-1410) by Gaston Phébus

Bibliotèque Nationale, Paris

12 twelve squirrels

Abu'l Hasan (17th Century), *Squirrels in a Plane Tree* (about 1610)

The British Library, London

13 thirteen singers

Thomas Cooper Gotch (1854-1931), *Alleluia* (exhibited 1896)

The Tate Gallery, London

14 fourteen soldiers

Henri Rousseau (1844-1910), *Artillerymen* (about 1893-1895)

The Solomon R. Guggenheim Museum, New York

Gift of Solomon R. Guggenheim

15 fifteen hands and feet

Fernand Léger (1881-1955), *Divers on a Yellow Background* (1941)

The Art Institute of Chicago

Gift of Mr. and Mrs. Maurice Culberg

16 sixteen apples

Lucas Cranach the Elder (1472-1553), *Madonna and Child under an Apple Tree*

Hermitage Museum, St. Petersburg

17 seventeen birds

Pablo Picasso (1881-1973), *The New Year* (1953)

Saint-Denis Musée d'Art et d'Histoire, Paris

18 eighteen cherries

Georg Flegel (1566-1638), *Still Life*

Private Collection

19 nineteen stars

Robert Indiana (born 1928), *The American Dream I* (1961)

The Museum of Modern Art, New York

Gift of The Larry Aldrich Foundation Fund

20 twenty angels

Sandro Botticelli (about 1445-1510), *Mystic Nativity* (1500)

The National Gallery, London

ACKNOWLEDGEMENTS

The author and publishers would like to thank the galleries, museums, private collectors and copyright holders who have given their permission to reproduce the pictures in this book.

Swabian School, *Portrait of a Woman of the Hofer Family*,
Jan van Huijsum, *Flowers in a Terracotta Vase*,
Sandro Botticelli, *Mystic Nativity*, The Trustees, The National Gallery, London
Karel Appel, *Cry for Freedom*, © Karel Appel
c/o De Tulp Pers 1993/N.V. Koninklijke Bijenkorf Beheer KBB, Amsterdam.
Paul Gauguin, *Still Life with Three Puppies*, Oil on wood, 91.8 x 62.6cm.
Photograph © 1992 The Museum of Modern Art, New York
Henri Matisse, *Goldfish*, © Succession H. Matisse/D.A.C.S. 1993,
photograph: Bridgeman Art Library, London
Utagawa Kuniyoshi, *Boat Trip in Winter*, Vincent Van Gogh, *Boats on the Beach*,
Vincent Van Gogh Foundation/Van Gogh Museum, Amsterdam
Wassily Kandinsky, *Swinging*, © A.D.A.G.P., Paris and D.A.C.S., London 1993
Studio of Peter Paul Rubens, *The Gerbier Family*, © H. M. The Queen
Sir Stanley Spencer, *St. Francis and the Birds*, © Estate of Stanley Spencer 1993
All rights reserved D.A.C.S.
Abu'l Hasan, *Squirrels in a Plane Tree*, By permission of the British Library
Thomas Cooper Gotch, *Alleluia*, photograph: John Webb
Henri Rousseau, *Artillerymen,* photograph: David Heald
© The Solomon R. Guggenheim Foundation, New York, 1993
Fernand Léger, French, *Divers on a Yellow Background*,
photograph courtesy of The Art Institute of Chicago/© D.A.C.S. 1993
Lucas Cranach, *Madonna and Child under an Apple Tree*,
photograph: Bridgeman Art Library, London
Pablo Picasso, *The New Year*, © D.A.C.S. 1993
Georg Flegel, *Still Life*, © Christie's 1993
Robert Indiana, *The American Dream I,* Oil on canvas, 183 x 152.7cm.
Photograph © 1992 The Museum of Modern Art, New York

Other titles in the series

I Spy – An Alphabet in Art
I Spy – Animals in Art
I Spy – Shapes in Art
I Spy – Colours in Art

First published in Great Britain by HarperCollins Publishers Ltd in 1993
This edition published by HarperCollins Children's Books in 2004

20
ISBN-13: 978-0-00-664298-5

Visit our website at: www.harpercollins.co.uk

Printed in China